Animal Teams

Wolf Packs

by Lisa Bullard

FOCUS READERS

BEACON

www.focusreaders.com

Focus Readers is distributed by North Star Editions:
sales@northstareditions.com | 888-417-0195

Produced for Focus Readers by Red Line Editorial.

Photographs ©: Shutterstock Images, cover, 1, 4, 6, 8, 10, 12, 14–15, 16, 18, 21, 22, 25, 26, 29

Library of Congress Cataloging-in-Publication Data
Names: Bullard, Lisa, author.
Title: Wolf packs / by Lisa Bullard.
Description: Mendota Heights, MN: Focus Readers, [2025] | Series: Animal teams | Includes bibliographical references and index. | Audience: Grades 2-3
Identifiers: LCCN 2023059371 (print) | LCCN 2023059372 (ebook) | ISBN 9798889981954 (hardcover) | ISBN 9798889982517 (paperback) | ISBN 9798889983606 (pdf) | ISBN 9798889983071 (ebook)
Subjects: LCSH: Wolves--Juvenile literature. | Wolves--Behavior--Juvenile literature. | Wolves--Life cycles--Juvenile literature.
Classification: LCC QL737.C22 B8355 2025 (print) | LCC QL737.C22 (ebook) | DDC 599.77--dc23/eng/20240125
LC record available at https://lccn.loc.gov/2023059371
LC ebook record available at https://lccn.loc.gov/2023059372

Printed in the United States of America
Mankato, MN
082024

About the Author

Lisa Bullard is the author of more than 100 books for children, including the mystery novel *Turn Left at the Cow*. She also teaches writing classes for adults and children. Lisa grew up in Minnesota, and now lives just north of Minneapolis.

Table of Contents

Chapter 1

Howling Together

A group of wolves stands silently in the forest. Suddenly, the biggest wolf throws back his head. He howls. The sound pierces the air. Before it fades, a second wolf joins in. Then a third wolf joins, too.

Wolves can start howling when they are just a few weeks old.

Touching muzzles can be a friendly action.

Other packmates add their voices. The **chorus** rings through the trees.

The pack starts to move. One wolf licks another's **muzzle**. Another wolf wags his tail. Some packmates sniff and rub each other. Others wrestle on the ground. Meanwhile, the howls continue. Even the wolf pups add tiny wails.

After a minute, the wolves stop howling. Their shared song was fun. It helped the pack **bond**. Now it's time to keep moving through the forest.

A wolf pack's howls can be heard up to 10 miles (16 km) away.

Chapter 2

Raising Pups

Wolves are **social** animals. They live together in packs. Wolf packs come in different sizes. Many packs have 10 wolves or fewer. But some packs have up to 30 wolves.

Wolves live in North America, Europe, and Asia.

Most litters have four to six pups.

Packs are based on family groups. Each pack is run by a **breeding pair**. These wolves are the parents of many pack members. The two **mate**. The mother wolf has a new litter of pups each year.

Packs often include other family members, too. The pups' aunts, uncles, or grandparents could be there. And sometimes, packs take in outsiders. That way, those wolves do not have to live alone.

At first, pups drink their mother's milk. But after a month, many packmates help feed the pups. When a pup wants food, it licks an older wolf's muzzle. Then the older wolf throws up. The pup eats the food from the older wolf's stomach.

Pups are usually born in spring or early summer. Later in summer, they are big enough to play.

Packmates care for pups in other ways, too. They babysit while the mother wolf hunts. Packmates sometimes bring the pups toys. These include sticks and bones.

Older wolves play with the pups. That helps pups learn their role in the pack. It also helps teach the pups hunting skills.

When pups are grown, some stay with the pack. Others leave. They can form packs of their own. Then they will take care of their new family.

Wolves usually stay with the same mates for life.

Caring for All

Wolves care for more than just pups. They help other packmates, too. Some older wolves are not strong enough to hunt. But they still get food. The pack lets them eat from their shared food.

New mothers often need help, too. After giving birth, they have to stay close to their pups. So, packmates bring them food. Other times, wolves get hurt while hunting. They need to rest and heal. Those wolves can share the pack's food, too.

Hurt wolves may have trouble walking or running.

Chapter 3

Hunting as a Team

Animals with hooves are wolves' main **prey**. These animals include deer, elk, and caribou. They are often large and travel in big groups. Wolf packs use teamwork to hunt the big animals.

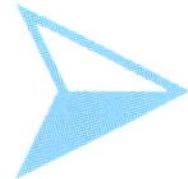

One deer can feed a pack of wolves for several days.

Some wolves can run more than 35 miles per hour (56 km/h).

Packs sometimes follow big animals for long distances. Wolves make plans during this time. They see their prey getting tired. The wolves watch for weaker animals. They study the land, too. Wolves move easily over deep snow. So, they might wait until the prey moves into snowy areas.

When the time is right, some wolves move in to attack. Each wolf has a job. The jobs are based on the wolves' sizes and skills. Smaller female wolves are often fastest. They run ahead. They separate a weak animal from the herd. They bite at it from the back.

Male wolves are stronger. Males often bite prey in the throat. They bring the animal to the ground. Half-grown pups watch from the side. Watching is how they learn.

This teamwork helps the pack catch more prey. But wolves might hunt in packs for another reason,

Wolves might go days without eating. But they can eat up to 20 pounds (9.1 kg) of food at once.

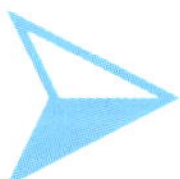

Sometimes ravens lead wolves to prey and then steal some of the food after the kill is made.

too. Animals such as ravens try to steal their kills. The wolves can lose a lot of food to these **scavengers**. Larger packs can guard the food more easily.

Chapter 4

Guarding the Land

Each wolf pack usually has its own **territory**. Some territories are larger than others. A pack in a cold northern place might need more land. Prey there might be more spread out.

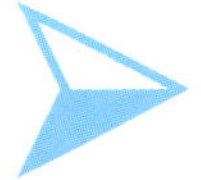

Wolves might have to travel long distances to find prey.

Defending their territory is important to a pack. Wolves need to guard their food sources. If too many animals take a pack's prey, the pack may go hungry. And the pack has to keep pups safe, too. Packmates work and fight together to protect their home area.

Wolves often warn other packs to stay away. For example, they use scents from their bodies to mark the territory's edges. Packs also howl together to warn other wolves.

Rolling can help a wolf pick up scents from the ground.

While howling, some wolves change the tone of their howls. That can make a pack sound bigger than it really is.

A wolf has a very powerful bite. That helps it fight or catch prey.

Sometimes wolf packs fight over territory. Wolves can be hurt or killed. Fights are one of the biggest killers of wild wolves. In a fight, the bigger pack often wins. But that's not the only thing that makes a difference. Often, the pack with more older wolves wins. Older wolves have more experience. They are trained fighters and good leaders. That makes them **crucial** members of any pack. Strong packs defend their land well. The whole group can live together safely.

If a packmate is in trouble, another wolf might jump in to help. Wolves do this even if it puts them in danger.

FOCUS ON

Wolf Packs

Write your answers on a separate piece of paper.

1. Write a few sentences describing how the whole pack helps take care of wolf pups.
2. What behavior of wolf packs is most interesting to you? Why?
3. What is one kind of prey that wolves eat?
   - A. other wolves
   - B. ravens
   - C. deer
4. Why do wolf packs target weaker prey?
   - A. Weaker prey taste better than stronger prey.
   - B. Weaker prey are slower and easier to catch.
   - C. Weaker prey are easier to smell.

5. What does **litter** mean in this book?

The two mate. The mother wolf has a new ***litter*** *of pups each year.*

A. a very old wolf
B. a group of baby wolves
C. a breeding pair

6. What does **experience** mean in this book?

Often, the pack with more older wolves wins. Older wolves have more ***experience****. They are trained fighters and good leaders.*

A. fear of fighting
B. knowledge based on doing something before
C. lack of practice

Answer key on page 32.

Glossary

bond
To form a close relationship.

breeding pair
The two wolves, a male and a female, who are in charge of a pack.

chorus
The sound of many voices howling together.

crucial
Very important.

mate
To come together in order to have babies.

muzzle
An animal's nose and mouth.

prey
Animals that are hunted and eaten by other animals.

scavengers
Animals that eat dead and decaying remains of living things.

social
Likely to spend time with other animals of the same type.

territory
An area that is defended by a group of animals.

To Learn More

BOOKS

Markle, Sandra. *On the Hunt with Wolves.* Minneapolis: Lerner Publications, 2023.

Rathburn, Betsy. *Arctic Wolves.* Minneapolis: Bellwether Media, 2021.

Schuh, Mari. *Wolves.* North Mankato, MN: Capstone, 2020.

NOTE TO EDUCATORS

Visit **www.focusreaders.com** to find lesson plans, activities, links, and other resources related to this title.

Index

Answer Key: 1. Answers will vary; **2.** Answers will vary; **3.** C; **4.** B; **5.** B; **6.** B